SCIENCE HIGHLIG

1800-1900
THE ADVENT OF ELECTRICITY

By Charlie Samuels

Gareth Stevens
Publishing

Please visit our Web site www.garethstevens.com. For a free color catalog of all our high-quality books, call toll free 1-800-542-2595 or fax 1-877-542-2596.

Library of Congress Cataloging-in-Publication Data
Samuels, Charlie, 1961-
  The advent of electricity (1800-1900) / Charlie Samuels.
    p. cm. — (Science highlights)
  Includes index.
  ISBN 978-1-4339-4148-1 (lib. bdg.)
  ISBN 978-1-4339-4149-8 (pbk.)
  ISBN 978-1-4339-4150-4 (6-pack)
  1. Electricity--Juvenile literature. 2. Electricity--Experiments—History—19th century—Juvenile literature. I. Title.
  QC527.2.S26 2011
  537.09'034—dc22

                          2010013221

Published in 2011 by
Gareth Stevens Publishing
111 East 14th Street, Suite 349
New York, NY 10003

© 2011 The Brown Reference Group Ltd.

For Gareth Stevens Publishing:
Art Direction: Haley Harasymiw
Editorial Direction: Kerri O'Donnell

For The Brown Reference Group Ltd:
Editorial Director: Lindsey Lowe
Managing Editor: Tim Cooke
Children's Publisher: Anne O'Daly
Design Manager: David Poole
Designer: Kim Browne
Picture Manager: Sophie Mortimer
Production Director: Alastair Gourlay

Picture Credits
Front Cover: Science Photo Library: Peter Menzel

Inside: iStockphoto: 31br; **Jupiter:** Stockxpert 21; **Public Domain:** Les Fossiles – Empreinte des Mondes Disparus 7tl; **Shutterstock:** Awe Inspiring Images 43r, James Cox 17t, Alexander Kaths 27, Sebastian Kaulitzki 5, 30, Kateryna Larina 22, Mikhail Pogosov, 26, Tatiana Popova 40tr, Dr Morley Read 6, Sportgraphic 35; **Thinkstock:** AbleStock 7cr, Comstock 11tl, Photos.com 10, 11br, 14, 15, 18, 23, 31tl, 32t, 33, 38, 39, 44; **Topfoto:** 42, HIP 34, The Granger Collection 13;.

The Brown Reference Group has made every attempt to contact the copyright holders. If anyone has any information please contact info@brownreference.com

All Artwork The Brown Reference Group

Manufactured in the United States of America
1 2 3 4 5 6 7 8 9 12 11 10

CPSIA compliance information: Batch #CS10GS: For further information contact Gareth Stevens, New York, New York at 1-800-542-2595.

Contents

Introduction

The 19th century marked many scientific turning points. By its end, scientists had worked out the answers to problems that could still only be guessed at in 1800.

Where did humans come from? How did organisms inherit qualities from their parents? How old was Earth? What were the building blocks of substances? How did disease spread? And what was the nature of electricity? By 1900, researchers had come up with answers to such questions that are still largely accepted today. Many of the individual scientists were enthusiastic amateurs, as in earlier decades. By the end of the century, however, science was increasingly a specialized pursuit followed in laboratories by academics who were effectively professional scientists.

Theory and Practice

Many of the developments covered in this book were theoretical. People made careful observations and studies and then developed a theory to explain them. Charles Darwin's theory of evolution, Gregor Mendel's theory of genetics, and Dmitri Mendeleyev's theories about the nature of elements could only be proved later, when scientific knowledge caught up with their insights. Other developments were practical, however, and few were as influential as the invention of the internal combustion engine, which would begin a transportation revolution and lead to the coming of not only the age of the motor car but also of the airplane.

About This Book

This book uses timelines to describe scientific and technological advances from about 1800 to about 1900. A continuous timeline of the period runs along the bottom of all the pages. Its entries are color-coded to indicate the different fields of science to which they belong. Each chapter also has a subject timeline, which runs vertically down the edge of the page.

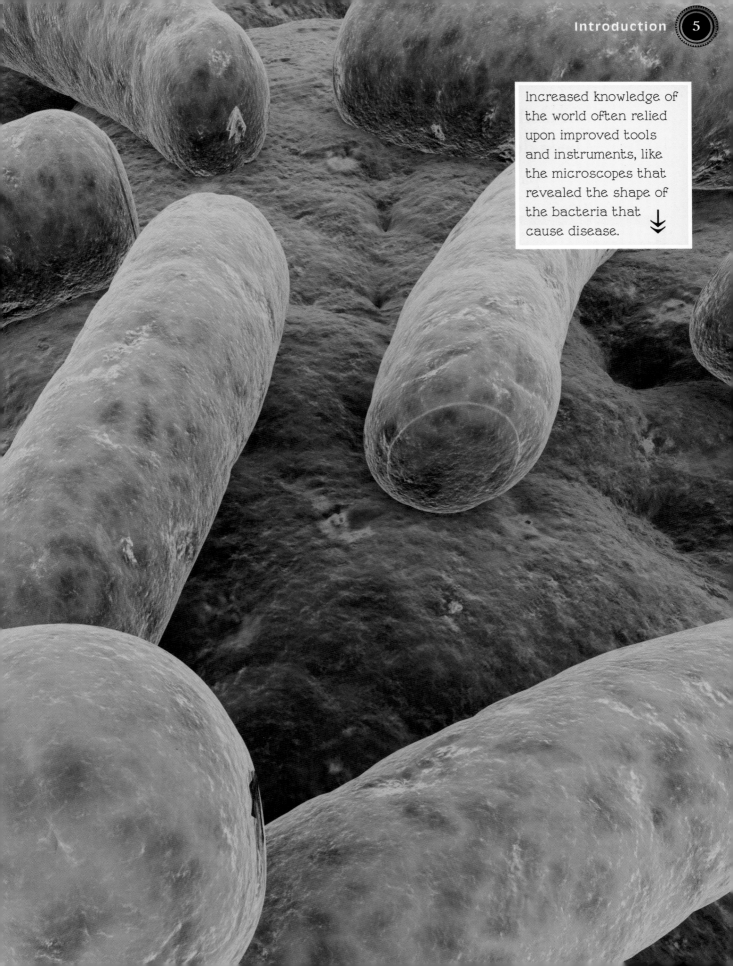

Increased knowledge of the world often relied upon improved tools and instruments, like the microscopes that revealed the shape of the bacteria that cause disease.

Evidence in Fossils

Fossils are the remains of plants and animals that have been dead for a very long time. They are usually the hard parts of animals that have been changed to rock.

↑ Trilobites are common fossils. The sea creatures died out 250 million years ago.

TIMELINE
1800–1805

KEY:

Astronomy and Math

Chemistry and Physics

Biology and Medicine

Inventions and Engineering

1800 English astronomer William Herschel discovers infrared radiation (from the sun).

1801 English physicist Thomas Young observes the interference of light.

1802 French naturalist Jean-Baptiste Lamarck introduces the word "biology" for the study of living things and life processes.

1800　　　　1801　　　　1802

1800 Italian astronomer Giuseppe Piazzi locates Ceres, the first asteroid (minor planet) to be discovered.

1800 Italian physicist Alessandro Volta invents the voltaic pile battery for producing a continuous electric current.

Mary Anning became one of the most successful 19th-century fossil hunters.

In 1517, the Italian physician and poet Girolamo Fracastoro was probably the first person to suggest that fossils are the remains of living organisms. But no one took much notice at the time, and it was not until the fossil finds in Europe of the late 18th century that scientists began to realize that fossils can tell us a great deal about the history of living things and the rocks in which they are found.

In 1793, French naturalist Jean-Baptiste Lamarck (1744–1829) revived the idea that fossils represent ancient organisms, and this time other scientists began to listen to the argument. Two years later, another Frenchman, Georges Cuvier (1769–1832), discovered one of the first dinosaur fossils, although the word "dinosaur," which comes from Greek words meaning "terrible lizard," only came later when the famous English fossil hunter Richard Owen (1804–1892) invented the term in 1842.

Timeline

1517 Fracastoro suggests fossils are animal remains

1793 Lamarck revives Fracastoro's theory

1795 Cuvier discovers a dinosaur fossil

1811 Mary Anning discovers ichthyosaur fossil

1816 William Smith proposes fossil–rock date correlation

Ancient dinosaur bones preserved in stone.

1803 English chemist John Dalton proposes his atomic theory: that elements are made up of indivisible atoms that combine to form chemical compounds.

1804 English inventor and founder of the science of aerodynamics George Cayley builds and flies a model glider.

1803   1804   1805

1803 English engineer Richard Trevithick makes the first steam-powered railroad locomotive.

1803 German physician John Otto describes the inherited blood disorder hemophilia.

1805 French inventor Joseph Jacquard constructs a loom that is controlled by a "chain" of punched cards.

Mary Anning, Fossil Hunter

As sea cliffs become eroded by waves and weather, the sedimentary rocks release any fossils they contain. In 1811, schoolgirl Mary Anning was walking on a beach in Dorset, southern England, when she found a complete fossil skeleton of an ichthyosaur, a fishlike reptile that swam in the seas 150 million years ago during the Mesozoic Era. The enterprising 12-year-old sold her find to a museum and went on to become one of the world's best-known fossil collectors.

How Fossils Form

Paleontologists (scientists who study fossils) discovered several ways in which fossils can form. Animal remains need to be buried quickly, before the carcass can decay or be eaten by scavengers. The best place for that to happen is underwater, in the mud or sediment at the bottom of a lake or sea. That is also the place where sedimentary rocks form. Remains embedded in sediment may be dissolved by water, leaving behind a perfect mold. Minerals may be deposited in the mold, forming a cast often made from a totally different type of rock than the sediment. Footprints or animal tracks in mud can be preserved in a similar way. Preserving a whole animal only happens occasionally when conditions are right, as when insects become trapped in amber (fossilized tree resin) or mammoths are buried in the permanently frozen ground of the permafrost. (Sometimes, even human skeletons have been fossilized. Tar pits in California have preserved some complete skeletons of prehistoric animals.

1

2

3

4

TIMELINE
1805–1810

KEY:

- Astronomy and Math
- Chemistry and Physics
- Biology and Medicine
- Inventions and Engineering

1805 French naturalist Georges Cuvier founds the science of comparative anatomy.

1806 French chemists identify the first amino acid, asparagine (in asparagus).

1807 U.S. engineer Robert Fulton builds a successful paddle steamer, *Clermont*.

1805

1806

1807

1805 English naval officer Francis Beaufort devises the Beaufort scale for classifying the strength of winds.

1806 Swiss mathematician Jean-Robert Argand devises the Argand diagram for representing complex numbers as points on a coordinate plane.

1807 The Royal Geological Society is founded in London.

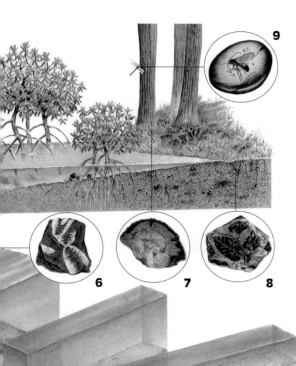

1. **Coral skeletons (form reefs)**

2. **Silica skeleton of zooplankton**

3. **Ammonite shell**

4. **Bivalve (mollusk) shell**

5. **Trace fossils of tracks in mud**

6. **Graptolite (planktonlike) fossils**

7. **Petrified wood from tree**

8. **Carbonized leaves**

9. **Insect trapped in amber**

↑ An artist's reconstruction shows a sequence of fossil formation.

Using Fossils for Dating

Over millions of years, sedimentary rocks form strata one above the other. As long as no great upheavals disturb them, younger rock layers always lie on top of older ones. In 1816, geologist William Smith showed that the age of a fossil must be the same as that of the rock in which it is found (and vice versa). This provided a new method of geological dating. Absolute dating of fossils and rocks had to await 20th-century techniques such as dating by radioactivity.

1808 English chemist Humphry Davy invents the arc lamp.

1809 French naturalist Jean-Baptiste Lamarck proposes the (now discredited) theory that acquired characteristics, such as a weightlifter's muscles, are passed on from parents to their offspring.

1808   1809   1810

1808 French physicist Siméon Poisson puts forward a theory to account for irregularities in the orbits of the planets.

1808 English inventor George Cayley builds an unmanned glider.

1810 French chef Nicolas Appert invents food canning (originally for Napoleon's army).

The Birth of Photography

The camera had its beginnings nearly 1,000 years before film, which had to await the discovery of light-sensitive chemicals that could "capture" the camera's image.

⟫ In 1843, William Fox Talbot set up a photographic "factory" in his greenhouse.

TIMELINE
1810–1815

KEY:

- Astronomy and Math
- Chemistry and Physics
- Biology and Medicine
- Inventions and Engineering

1811 English astronomer William Herschel proposes a theory that stars develop from nebulas as clouds of gas condense into star clusters.

1811 Italian scientist Amedeo Avogadro proposes Avogadro's law: that at the same temperature and pressure, equal volumes of all gases contain the same number of molecules.

1810   1811   1812

1810 German engineer Friedrich König invents a steam-powered printing press.

1811 Schoolgirl Mary Anning discovers the first fossil of an ichthyosaur in southern England.

The origin of the camera was the camera obscura (Latin for "dark room"), a windowless room with a small hole in one wall. Light entering the hole forms an upside-down image of the scene outside on the opposite wall. Artists used the device as an aid to trace an image, and later it became portable in the form of a large light-excluding box. In this version, a glass lens soon replaced the hole.

↑ Early cameras were clumsy to use; they had to be large to hold photographic plates.

Fixing an Image on Paper

In 1725, the German physician Johann Schulze found that certain silver salts turn dark when exposed to daylight. Fifty years later, Swedish chemist Karl Scheele discovered that the darkening effect is due to the presence of grains of metallic silver. As a result, silver salts were to become standard ingredients in photographic emulsions (light-sensitive coatings) for films, paper, and even leather—as tried in the late 1790s by Englishman Thomas Wedgwood.

Timeline

1725 Light sensitivity of silver salts

1826 Niépce's first photograph

1839 Daguerreotypes

1841 Calotypes

1851 Wet-collodion process

1871 Dry gelatin plates

1888 First Kodak camera

↑ An artist uses a camera obscura to re-create an outdoor scene indoors.

1813 Swiss botanist Augustin de Candolle devises a plant classification system, which he calls a "taxonomy."

1814 German physicist Joseph von Fraunhofer invents the spectroscope.

1813

1814

1815

1813 English engineer William Hedley builds his steam locomotive *Puffing Billy*.

1814 Spanish-born physician Matthieu Orfila founds the modern science of toxicology, the study of poisons.

1815 French physicist Augustin-Jean Fresnel discovers the diffraction of light as it passes through a small aperture.

How a Camera Obscura Works

In a portable camera obscura, a lens focuses light from a scene onto a mirror. The mirror, angled at 45 degrees, reflects the image upward onto a glass screen. An artist can then trace the image. This method may have been used by the painter Canaletto, who made detailed cityscapes. The camera obscura was used as an artist's aid until it was replaced by photographs after the 1850s.

→ The portable camera obscura was a box fitted with a lens and a mirror.

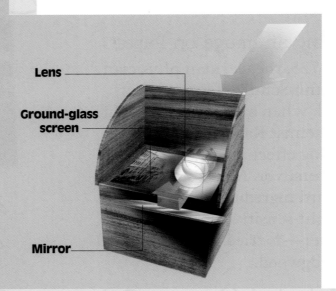

Lens

Ground-glass screen

Mirror

In France, Joseph Niépce experimented with fleeting silver images. His first successful photograph in 1826 used a polished pewter plate coated with bitumen as the light-sensitive substance.

In 1839, Frenchman Louis Daguerre used iodine to make photographic plates. He exposed the plate in a camera and "developed" it in mercury vapor. The image was made permanent, or "fixed," in a solution of common salt. These daguerreotypes, as his images were known, were mirror images and were used only once.

A Series of Improvements

In 1841, English chemist William Fox Talbot patented his calotype process. After exposure to light in a camera, the film was developed in a solution of gallic acid and fixed. The resulting "negative" image (with black and white reversed) was placed with a sheet of light-sensitive paper and changed back to positive. This stage could be repeated many times.

TIMELINE
1815–1820

1815 English geologist William Smith publishes a geological map of the rocks of England and Wales.

1815 In England, chemist Humphry Davy and engineer George Stephenson independently invent a safety lamp for miners.

KEY:

- Astronomy and Math
- Chemistry and Physics
- Biology and Medicine
- Inventions and Engineering

1815

1816

1817

1815 English scholar Peter Roget devises a slide rule with two logarithmic scales to help with multiplication and division.

1816 Scottish engineer Robert Stirling invents a two-cylinder external combustion engine.

1817 French chemists discover chlorophyll, the light-absorbing pigment in plants.

Fox Talbot established himself as one of the world's first professional photographers, with a studio in Reading, southern England, where the rich and famous had their portraits taken between 1843 and 1847. The texture of the paper meant the prints remained slightly coarse. Frenchman Louis-Désiré Blanquart-Evrard made more improvements in 1850 by coating the printing paper with albumen (egg white).

A Londoner, Frederick Archer, invented the wet-collodion process in 1851. It was used until dry plates, using gelatin emulsions, superseded it in the late 1870s. American George Eastman used a dry gelatin emulsion for his first Kodak camera of 1888, initially on paper film and a year later on transparent celluloid. With the Kodak, the era of mass-market photography had arrived.

⬆ This daguerreotype of a street in Paris, made by Daguerre in 1839, is the first ever photograph to include a human being.

1818 German-born English engineer Rudolph Ackermann devises a steering mechanism for horse-drawn carriages; it remains the basis of modern automobile steering.

1819 British astronomer John Herschel discovers that sodium thiosulfate can "fix" a newly developed photographic image.

1820 The Royal Astronomical Society is founded in London.

1818

1819

1820

1819 U.S. engineers Stephen McCormick and Jethro Wood independently produce a cast-iron plow.

1819 German inventor Augustus Siebe develops a pressurized diving suit complete with helmet.

Michael Faraday

Faraday was a physicist and a chemist, one of the greatest experimental scientists who ever lived. He founded the sciences of electromagnetism and electrochemistry.

→→ Faraday's Christmas lectures presented science in a simple way to nonscientific audiences.

TIMELINE
1820–1825

KEY:

- Astronomy and Math
- Chemistry and Physics
- Biology and Medicine
- Inventions and Engineering

1820 Danish physicist Hans Ørsted discovers electromagnetism when he notices the needle of a compass is deflected by an electric current.

1821 French astronomer Alexis Bouvard observes irregularities in the orbit of Uranus; they prove to be caused by the gravity of Neptune.

1822 Charles Babbage makes a mechanical adding machine, or "difference engine."

1820

1821

1822

1820 French chemists discover the alkaloid quinine, soon to be used to treat malaria.

1821 U.S. engineer Zachariah Allen installs the first hot-air central heating system.

1822 French naturalist Jean-Baptiste Lamarck distinguishes between vertebrates and invertebrates.

Michael Faraday, the son of a blacksmith, was born just outside London. At 13, he left school to become an apprentice bookbinder. Reading some of the books stirred in him an interest in science. He even carried out simple experiments with electricity. In 1813, he became assistant to English chemist Humphry Davy at the Royal Institution, where part of his job was to set up experiments for Davy's lectures. In 1827, he took over Davy's post of lecturer at the Royal Institution, becoming professor of chemistry there in 1833.

Chemical Discoveries

Faraday made several discoveries in chemistry. In 1823, he liquefied chlorine by heating it in a sealed tube; previously only two other gases had been liquefied. In 1825, Faraday discovered benzene. In 1834, he turned his attention to electrolysis, the process in which an electric current passing through a solution (electrolyte) between two electrodes brings about chemical change. Usually a gas

Timeline
1821 Simple electric motor

1823 Liquid chlorine

1825 Benzene

1831 Electromagnetic induction

1834 Laws of electrolysis

← Michael Faraday is shown here in his role as a chemist. His most important discovery was that of benzene, the first of the so-called aromatic hydrocarbons and the basis of a new branch of organic chemistry.

1823 Scottish chemist Charles Macintosh patents waterproof fabric made by impregnating cloth with rubber.

1824 French physicist Dominique Arago discovers magnetic induction—the production of an electric field by a changing magnetic field.

1823   1824   1825

1823 The medical journal *The Lancet* is published for the first time in London.

1824 Swedish chemist Jöns Berzelius discovers silicon; a year later Danish physicist Hans Ørsted prepares an impure form of aluminum.

1825 The Stockton and Darlington Railway, the first regular commercial steam railroad, opens in northern England.

Magnetic Fields

Surrounding every magnet is a field of force known as a magnetic field. Faraday studied the interaction between such fields and electric currents flowing in wires and other conductors. This branch of physics is now called electromagnetism. It is the basis of most electrical machines, from motors and dynamos to the electric bell, the relay, and the solenoid (a type of electric switch).

→ The angle of the coil dictates whether or not a magnetic field produces a turning force (top) or not (below).

is produced at either electrode, or a metal is deposited on the negatively charged cathode. The experiments led to Faraday's laws of electrolysis: 1. The amount of chemical change is proportional to the quantity of electricity; 2. The amount of change (produced by a fixed quantity of electricity) in different substances is proportional to the equivalent weight of the substance.

The Electric Motor

In physics, Faraday made the first primitive electric motor in 1821. He suspended a length of stiff wire next to a bar magnet that projected vertically from a dish of mercury. When he connected a battery between the mercury and the top of the wire, the lower end of the

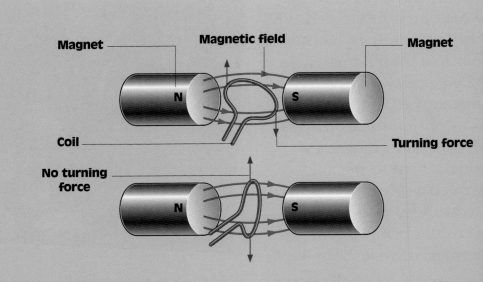

TIMELINE
1825–1830

KEY:

- Astronomy and Math
- Chemistry and Physics
- Biology and Medicine
- Inventions and Engineering

1825 French naturalist Georges Cuvier puts forward his catastrophe theory of extinction, that cataclysmic events cause species to become extinct.

1826 French chemist Joseph Niépce takes the first photograph (on a metal plate).

1827 U.S. artist John James Audubon publishes the first pa of *Birds of America*.

1825   1826   1827

1825 English chemist and physicist Michael Faraday discovers benzene and several of its compounds.

1826 German astronomer Heinrich Olbers puts forward his famous paradox: Why is the sky dark at night when the universe is full of stars?

wire rotated around the magnet. In 1831, Faraday wound two separate coils of wire around an iron ring. He connected one wire to a galvanometer (an instrument that detects an electric current). When he connected a battery to the other wire, the galvanometer needle registered a current. He also showed that when a magnet is moved in and out of a wire coil, a current is generated in the coil. Faraday had discovered the phenomenon of electromagnetic induction.

Faraday made many lasting contributions, including the children's Christmas lectures, which he started at the Royal Institution in 1826 and which he continued for 19 years. His "The Chemical History of a Candle" is still published, and eminent scientists still give the lectures. Faraday's name is commemorated in two scientific units. The farad is the SI unit of capitance, and the Faraday constant is the electric charge carried by 1 mole of electrons or singly charged ions.

↑ The candle was the subject of one of Faraday's most popular lectures.

The Principle of the Electric Motor

Faraday demonstrated the principle of the electric motor with this simple apparatus. A copper rod, pivoted at the top, dips into a pool of mercury alongside a vertical magnet. When a current flows along the rod, the rod rotates around the magnet.

Battery
Copper rod
Magnet
Mercury

1828 French physiologist Pierre Flourens explains how the semicircular canals in the inner ear control the sense of balance.

1829 Blind French teacher Louis Braille invents the Braille alphabet to allow blind people to read.

1828

1829

1830

1828 Estonian naturalist Karl von Baer founds the science of embryology.

1829 George Stephenson's *Rocket* locomotive wins trials to provide the power for the Liverpool & Manchester Railway.

1830 U.S. engineer Peter Cooper builds *Tom Thumb*, the first locomotive to be made in North America.

Darwin and Evolution

In 1831, Charles Darwin set sail on HMS *Beagle*; during the voyage, the observations he made eventually led to his theory of evolution through natural selection.

◄◄ Darwin plays with a monkey companion in this cartoon. Darwin's idea that humans were descended from apes was widely mocked in popular magazines.

TIMELINE
1830–1835

KEY:

- Astronomy and Math
- Chemistry and Physics
- Biology and Medicine
- Inventions and Engineering

1830 Scottish writer Mary Somerville publishes a book of popular astronomy, *The Mechanism of the Heavens*.

1831 English scientist Michael Faraday makes a simple dynamo.

1832 French chemist Pierre Robiquet discovers codeine (in opium from poppies).

1830   1831   1832

1830 Scottish chemist Andrew Ure invents the bimetallic strip thermostat.

1831 English naval officer James Ross locates the position of the magnetic north pole (which constantly changes).

harles Darwin (1809–1882), grandson of English physician Erasmus Darwin, was 22 years old when e joined HMS *Beagle*. The young man's duty was to rovide company for the ship's captain, because the onventions of the time did not allow the captain to ocialize with his officers or crew.

Darwin wanted to be a naturalist, and he used the ve-year voyage to study plants and animals in faraway aces. The ship visited islands off the west coast of frica before sailing around Cape Horn and up the estern coast of South America. It then stopped in the alápagos Islands before sailing across the Pacific to ahiti and New Zealand. It headed back to England by ay of Mauritius and South Africa. At each stop, arwin went ashore to observe local flora and fauna nd collect specimens of rocks, plants, and animals.

bserving the Animals

South America, Darwin spent more time on land han on the ship. He studied the rocks and geology of e places he visited as well. In Patagonia, he found a hore with a 19.6-foot-high (6-m) cliff containing some uge bones. They were too large to belong to any living eature. He observed that—apart from size—they esembled those of South American armadillos and oths. He realized that their giant ancestors had become xtinct, but why? Were they not fit enough to survive?

Timeline

1831–1836 Voyage of HMS *Beagle*

1838 Reads *An Essay on the Principle of Population* by Thomas Malthus

1858 Joint paper with naturalist Alfred Russel Wallace

1859 Publishes *On the Origin of Species*

The Galapagos Islands provided Darwin with much evidence for evolution.

1833 English mathematician Charles Babbage begins work on his "analytical engine," a type of mechanical computer (which he never finishes).

1834 English scientist Michael Faraday formulates the laws of electrolysis.

1833

1834

1835

1833 U.S. engineer bed Hussey invents a eaping machine.

1833 U.S. Army surgeon William Beaumont explains the role of gastric juices in digestion.

1834 U.S. engineer Cyrus McCormick patents a reaping and binding machine, an early form of combine harvester.

The Finches of the Galápagos Islands

In the Galápagos, Darwin found species of finches that differed only in coloration and the shapes of their beaks. The finches that ate seeds had short, stubby beaks, while birds that ate insects had long, thin beaks. Darwin deduced that they were variations of a species that had gradually evolved beaks appropriate to their chosen food.

➤➤ Finches 1, 3, and 4 have long beaks for eating insects; finch 2 is a fruit-eating species; and the beaks of finches 5 and 6 are best at tackling seeds.

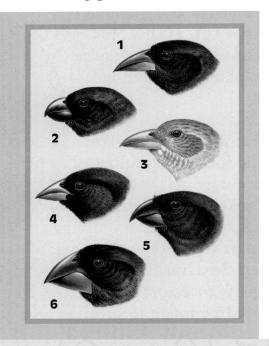

The *Beagle* returned to England in the fall of 1836, and Darwin moved to London. He studied geology and was converted to the ideas of geologist Charles Lyell, who argued the world was in a constant state of change

Forming a Theory

Darwin's main concern was animal species: what happens when species produce many offspring when there is insufficient food for all of them? Darwin's idea was that only the fittest animals survive, and that they did so because a process he called natural selection was taking place. "Nature"—that is, an individual's strength or adaptability—decided which animals survived.

At the same time Darwin was at work, Welsh naturalist Alfred Russel Wallace came to similar conclusions based on his observations of Asian and Australasian animals. He wrote about his theories in 1858 and sent them to Darwin. The pair consulted and issued a joint paper.

In 1859, Darwin published his epic *On the*

TIMELINE
1835–1840

KEY:

- Astronomy and Math
- Chemistry and Physics
- Biology and Medicine
- Inventions and Engineering

1835 U.S. manufacturer Samuel Colt produces a revolver with interchangeable parts.

1836 U.S. engineer Thomas Davenport makes a model streetcar.

1836 Swedish chemist Jöns Berzelius discovers catalysts, which speed up chemical reactions.

1835   1836   1837

1835 English photographer William Fox Talbot invents the calotype process, which produces paper negatives from which multiple photographic prints can be made.

1836 English naturalist Charles Darwin completes his voyage on HMS *Beagle*.

1837 U.S. industrialist John Deere invents a steel plow.

↑ The Galapagos were so remote that species had evolved there in isolation.

Origin of Species by Means of Natural Selection. He argued that evolution takes place in stages by chance mutations. Favorable mutations are inherited and passed on to offspring to produce a gradual change in a whole species. Eventually new, fitter species come into existence and old, less fit ones become extinct.

Darwin and his contemporaries had no idea exactly how mutations take place. Unknown to them, heredity was being studied in an Austrian monastery by the monk Gregor Mendel. He grew generations of pea plants to figure out the basic laws of heredity—how offspring receive sets of inherited "factors" that we now call genes. Genetics provides the means by which evolution takes place.

Darwin's Ideas and Human Society

Some thinkers tried to apply Darwin's theory of "the survival of the fittest" to human society. This theory, or Social Darwinism, argued that it was right that some people—the "fittest"—became successful while others remained poor. The theory was popular for a time, as it seemed to explain the wide differences between individuals' success and wealth. It was later rejected in favor of a more inclusive view, in which the rich help support the poor.

1838 French chemist Anselme Payen identifies cellulose, the basic material of all plants.

1839 U.S. inventor Charles Goodyear develops a process to harden rubber.

1838　　　　　1839　　　　　1840

1838 U.S. inventor Samuel Morse demonstrates his electric telegraph and the Morse code that it uses.

1839 French chemist Louis Daguerre invents the daguerreotype, a type of photograph taken on metal plates.

1839 German biologist Theodor Schwann suggests that all living matter is made up of cells.

Mendel and Genetics

Today, genetics is one of the major scientific disciplines. But it had humble beginnings in an Austrian monastery garden where Gregor Mendel grew pea plants.

← Genetics would eventually explain why family members look like one another.

TIMELINE
1840–1845

KEY:
- Astronomy and Math
- Chemistry and Physics
- Biology and Medicine
- Inventions and Engineering

1840 German pathologist Jacob Henle puts forward his germ theory of disease: that infection is caused by parasitic organisms invading the body.

1842 German physicist Julius von Mayer states the principle of the conservation of energy (that energy can be neither created nor destroyed, merely changed from one form to another).

1840   1841   1842

1840 German chemist Christian Schönbein discovers and names ozone.

1841 English engineer Joseph Whitworth introduces a system of standard screw threads.

1842 U.S. surgeon Crawford Long uses ether as an anesthetic.

Gregor Mendel (1822–1884) was born in Austrian Silesia (now the Czech Republic). He studied at college before becoming an Augustinian monk in 1843. He became interested in hybrids—plants grown by crossing two different species—and began to breed pea plants in 1856. Over the next six years he grew 30,000 plants, which he fertilized artificially by transferring pollen from one plant to another. For example, he crossed tall plants with short plants. He then counted the number of tall and short plants in the next and later generations. He found that all first-generation plants were tall, but the second generation had tall plants and short plants in the ratio of 3 to 1.

Factors of Inheritance

Mendel concluded that every plant receives two "factors" of inheritance, one from each parent. In the first generation of peas in the example, each plant receives one factor for tallness from the tall parent and one factor for shortness from the short parent. But all the offspring are tall since the tallness factor is dominant over the shortness factor (which is known as recessive). Recessive factors can become dominant when two occur in a single individual, as in short plants of the second generation.

⬆ Gregor Mendel's experiments with pea plants laid the foundations for the modern science of genetics.

1843 The world's first underwater tunnel is built beneath the Thames in London.

1844 U.S. dentist Horace Wells uses nitrous oxide ("laughing gas") as an anesthetic.

1845 German zoologist Karl Siebold shows that protozoa are single-celled organisms.

1843   1844   1845

1842 African-American inventor Norbert Rillieux designs a vacuum evaporator for extracting juice from sugarcane.

1844 U.S. inventor Samuel Morse sends the first message by telegraph in the United States.

1845 French physicists take detailed photographs of the sun.

The Calico Cat

Genes for black and ginger pigments are carried on the X chromosome. Black (B) is dominant over ginger (b). Females have two X chromosomes, so they can be black (BB), ginger (bb), or calico (Bb). Males have only one X (and one Y), so they can only be black (B) or ginger (b). Males can not be calico—which needs one black (B) and one ginger (b) allele—because they have only one X chromosome.

⟹ This diagram shows how calico cats get their mixture of black and ginger colors.

Mendel proposed two laws. The law of segregation states that the two factors controlling each hereditary characteristic segregate and pass into separate germ cells (egg and sperm). The law of independent assortment states that the pairs of factors segregate independently of each other during the formation of germ cells. He reported his results in 1865, publishing them a year later, but nobody took much notice at the time.

Building on Mendel's Work

Mendel's "factors" are now called alleles, which are alternative forms of a gene. There are two alleles of each gene in any cell, one inherited from each parent, which occupy the same place on a chromosome. Usually one allele is dominant, and the other is recessive. A germ cell (gamete)—egg or sperm—has one allele. When egg and sperm combine at fertilization, the two alleles come together in a new individual that

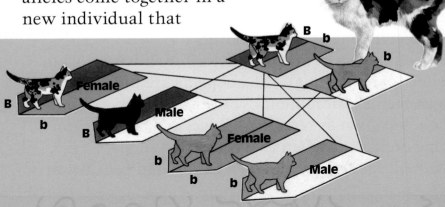

TIMELINE
1845–1850

KEY:
- Astronomy and Math
- Chemistry and Physics
- Biology and Medicine
- Inventions and Engineering

1845 German physicist Franz Neumann publishes his theory of electromagnetic induction.

1846 U.S. inventor Elias Howe invents a lock-stitch sewing machine.

1846 German astronomer Johann Galle is the first person to observe the planet Neptune.

1845   1846   1847

1845 British engineer Isambard Brunel launches the first successful propeller-driven ship, SS *Great Britain*.

1846 The Smithsonian Institution is founded in Washington, D.C.

1847 The American Medical Association is founded in Philadelphia.

>> Pea plants grow quickly, so Mendel was easily able to check his predictions.

nherits
haracteristics
rom each parent. The appearance
f the new individual depends on
rhich characteristic (if any) is
ominant.

After Mendel's death, several
iologists independently
:udied inheritance in plants.
n Holland, Hugo de Vries
ame up with identical results
> Mendel's, which he
nnounced in 1900. This led to
erman botanist Karl Correns
nd Austrian botanist Erich
on Tschermak-Seysenegg
ublishing their observations
nat confirmed Mendel had
een right.

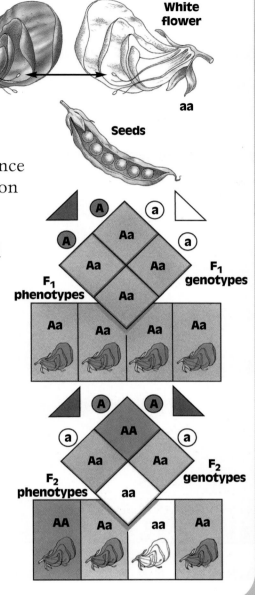

Purple flower
AA

White flower
aa

Seeds

A · a
F₁ phenotypes
A Aa a
Aa Aa
F₁ genotypes
Aa
Aa Aa Aa Aa

A · A
F₂ phenotypes
a AA a
Aa Aa
F₂ genotypes
aa
AA Aa aa Aa

Predicting Colors of Pea Plants

This diagram shows how Mendel's laws allow us to predict the colors that will be produced by crossing purple-flowered pea plants with white-flowered pea plants. Purple is dominant, and the first generation (known as F1 phenotypes) produced by planting seeds from the cross are all purple. But when this first generation is interbred in turn, the second generation (known as F2 phenotypes) has purple or white flowers in the ratio 3 purple to 1 white.

1848 Scottish physicist William Thomson, Lord Kelvin, introduces the absolute temperature (or Kelvin) scale.

1849 Swiss embryologist Rudolf von Kölliker states that nerve endings are extensions of nerve cells.

1848

1849

1850

1848 U.S. inventor James Bogardus introduces a method of making cast-iron buildings.

1849 Anglo-American engineer James Francis makes an improved reaction water turbine.

1850 English physician Alfred Higginson invents the hypodermic needle, initially for extracting samples of blood.

The Periodic Table

By 1869, following many new discoveries, there were 63 known chemical elements. From these, Dmitri Mendeleyev constructed his famous periodic table.

← Mendeleyev's periodic table later provided an insight into atomic structure.

TIMELINE
1850–1855

KEY:

- Astronomy and Math
- Chemistry and Physics
- Biology and Medicine
- Inventions and Engineering

ca 1850 German chemist Robert Bunsen begins using the Bunsen burner.

1851 French physicist Léon Foucault constructs Foucault's pendulum and uses it to prove the rotation of Earth.

1852 U.S. inventor Elisha Otis patents the safety elevator.

1850   1851   1852

1850 German physicist Rudolf Clausius formulates the second law of thermodynamics. It states that heat will not on its own move from a hot object to a hotter one.

1851 U.S. inventor Isaac Singer makes a single-thread sewing machine.

Russian chemist Dmitri Mendeleyev (1834–1907) was born in Tobolsk, Siberia, the youngest child of a large middle-class family. Despite the death of his father when Dmitri was 13, his mother was determined her youngest son should receive good schooling. He won a place at the Pedagogical Institute in St. Petersburg, a center for teacher training, qualifying as a teacher in 1855. He later studied chemistry at the University of St. Petersburg and in Germany. He took up a university post at St. Petersburg, and in 1869 began writing a textbook on chemistry (in those days inorganic chemistry).

Making the Table

Wishing to find order in the jumble of elements, he wrote the name of each on a card. He then dealt sets of "hands," like dealing out playing cards. He arranged the elements in order of increasing atomic weight (the average mass of an atom of the element). He saw that if he started a new row of cards every eighth element, those with similar chemical properties fell one above the other in columns.

Timeline

1869 Mendeleyev's periodic table

1875 Lecoq de Boisbaudran discovers gallium

1879 Nilson discovers scandium

1886 Winkler discovers germanium

1955 Discovery of mendelevium

Mendeleyev's work laid the foundations for all modern chemistry.

1854 English mathematician George Boole introduces Boolean algebra, later important in the development of computer circuits.

1854 U.S. chemist David Alter studies atomic spectra, the light given off by super-heated elements, and uses them as a method of chemical analysis.

1853

1854

1855

1853 English inventor George Cayley constructs a glider capable of carrying a person.

1854 British physician John Snow finds a link between cholera and contaminated drinking water in London.

1855 German pathologist Rudolph Virchow observes that cells originate from the division of other cells.

The Modern Periodic Table

Today's periodic table contains about 50 more elements than in Mendeleyev's time. They are arranged in order of their atomic numbers in seven horizontal "periods" of varying length. Two long series of 14 elements each—the lanthanides and the actinides—are shown in separate lines on page 29. The system of using a letter or letters to denote the symbol for each element (for example, Fe = iron) was introduced by Swedish chemist Jöns Berzelius (1779–1848) in 1818.

Mendeleyev saw that properties tended to recur along each row—there was a "periodicity" in the properties. He named his new grid of rows and columns the periodic table. He even included in the table additional "missing" elements that were still to be discovered. He predicted the chemical and physical properties of these elements, their atomic weights, and melting points.

In 1875, French chemist Paul Lecoq de Boisbaudran discovered "eka-aluminum" (in a space below aluminum), naming it gallium; in 1879, Swedish chemist Lars Nilson discovered "eka-boron"(below boron), and named it scandium; and in 1886, German chemist Clemens Winkler discovered "eka-silicon" (below silicon) and named it germanium. Mendeleyev's predictions had been fulfilled. By 1914, only seven gaps in the table remained up to element 92.

Atomic Structure

The atomic number is the total number of protons in an atom of any element. The modern periodic table is better described as being arranged in order of atomic number. In recent times, chemists have introduced the term "neutron number" (number of neutrons in the atom's nucleus) and call atomic weights "relative atomic masses." Mendeleyev could not explain the reason for the periodicity of the elements. That had to await an understanding of the structure of atoms, particularly

TIMELINE
1855–1860

KEY:

- Astronomy and Math
- Chemistry and Physics
- Biology and Medicine
- Inventions and Engineering

1855

1856

1857

1855 Italian physicist Luigi Palmieri designs a seismograph for measuring earthquakes.

1856 Remains of Neanderthal man are discovered by workmen in Germany.

1856 English steelmaker Henry Bessemer develops the Bessemer converter for making steel out of iron.

1855 English physicist John Pratt shows that gravity remains constant everywhere at sea level.

1856 English chemist William Perkin invents mauveine, the first synthetic dye, which becomes the basis of a huge industry.

1857 French chemist Louis Pasteur observes that microorganisms cause fermentation.

ow electrons arrange themselves around the nucleus of
n atom. In the 20th century, chemists realized that the
eriodic table reflected the atomic structures of the
ements as electrons fill up shells surrounding the
ucleus. The periodic table enables chemists to predict
ore accurately what reactions are possible. In 1955,
endeleyev received the ultimate honor when the
ement 101 was named mendelevium.

↓ Mendeleyev left gaps in the periodic table where he thought that elements would fit: all of those gaps have now been filled. New elements have also been added to the table.

1 **H** 1.0079																	2 **He** 4.0026
3 **Li** 6.941	4 **Be** 9.0122											5 **B** 10.811	6 **C** 12.011	7 **N** 14.0067	8 **O** 15.9994	9 **F** 18.9984	10 **Ne** 20.1797
11 **Na** 22.9898	12 **Mg** 24.3050											13 **Al** 26.9815	14 **Si** 28.0855	15 **P** 30.9738	16 **S** 32.066	17 **Cl** 35.4527	18 **Ar** 39.948
19 **K** 39.0983	20 **Ca** 40.078	21 **Sc** 44.9559	22 **Ti** 47.88	23 **V** 50.9415	24 **Cr** 51.9961	25 **Mn** 54.9380	26 **Fe** 55.847	27 **Co** 58.9332	28 **Ni** 58.6934	29 **Cu** 63.546	30 **Zn** 65.39	31 **Ga** 69.723	32 **Ge** 72.61	33 **As** 74.9216	34 **Se** 78.96	35 **Br** 79.904	36 **Kr** 83.80
37 **Rb** 85.4678	38 **Sr** 87.62	39 **Y** 88.9058	40 **Zr** 91.224	41 **Nb** 92.9064	42 **Mo** 95.94	43 **Tc** 98.9072	44 **Ru** 101.07	45 **Rh** 102.9055	46 **Pd** 106.42	47 **Ag** 107.8682	48 **Cd** 112.411	49 **In** 114.82	50 **Sn** 118.710	51 **Sb** 121.76	52 **Te** 121.757	53 **I** 126.0945	54 **Xe** 131.29
55 **Cs** 132.9054	56 **Ba** 137.327	57 **La** 138.9055	72 **Hf** 178.49	73 **Ta** 180.9479	74 **W** 183.85	75 **Re** 186.207	76 **Os** 190.2	77 **Ir** 192.22	78 **Pt** 195.08	79 **Au** 196.9665	80 **Hg** 200.59	81 **Tl** 204.3833	82 **Pb** 207.2	83 **Bi** 208.9804	84 **Po** 208.9824	85 **At** 209.9871	86 **Rn** 222.0176
87 **Fr** 223.0197	88 **Ra** 226.0254	89 **Ac** 227.0278	104 **Rf** 261.11	105 **Db** 262.114	106 **Sg** 263.118	107 **Bh** 262.12	108 **Hs** (265)	109 **Mt** (266)	110 **Uun** (269)	111 **Uuu** (272)	112 **Uub** (277)		114 **Uuq** (285)		116 **Uuh** (289)		118 **Uuo** (293)

Atomic number

nthanide series	58 **Ce** 140.115	59 **Pr** 140.9076	60 **Nd** 144.24	61 **Pm** 144.9127	62 **Sm** 150.36	63 **Eu** 151.965	64 **Gd** 157.25	65 **Tb** 158.9253	66 **Dy** 162.50	67 **Ho** 164.9303	68 **Er** 167.26	69 **Tm** 168.9342	70 **Yb** 173.04

29
Cu
63.546

													71 **Lu** 174.967
ctinide series	90 **Th** 222.0381	91 **Pa** 223.0359	92 **U** 238.0289	93 **Np** 237.0482	94 **Pu** 244.0642	95 **Am** 243.0614	96 **Cm** 247.0703	97 **Bk** 247.0703	98 **Cf** 251.0796	99 **Es** 252.083	100 **Fm** 257.0951	101 **Md** 258.10	102 **No** 259.1009
													103 **Lr** 262.11

Chemical symbol of element

Atomic weight

1858 English anatomist Henry Gray publishes his famous book, *Anatomy of the Human Body*, or *Gray's Anatomy*.

1859 Charles Darwin publishes *On the Origin of Species*, the book in which he puts forward his theory of evolution.

1858 — 1859 — 1860 →

1858 The first transatlantic submarine telegraph cable is laid.

1859 The world's first productive oil well is drilled in Pennsylvania by Edwin Drake.

1859 German chemist Hermann Kolbe synthesizes salicylic acid, leading to the mass production of the first synthetic drug, aspirin.

Germs and Disease

During the middle of the 19th century, scientists finally realized that germs cause most diseases and no longer blamed "evil spirits" or "bad air."

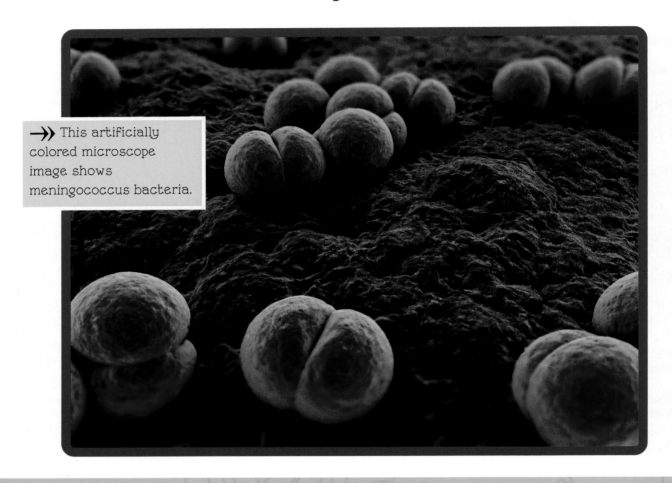

⟶ This artificially colored microscope image shows meningococcus bacteria.

TIMELINE
1860–1865

KEY:

Astronomy and Math

Chemistry and Physics

Biology and Medicine

Inventions and Engineering

1860 German scientists Robert Bunsen and Gustav Kirchhoff develop a method of analyzing substances by their spectra.

1861 In Australia, the first large-scale food-freezing plant is built to prepare meat for export to Britain.

1862 Swedish astronomer Anders Angström uses a spectroscope to identify hydrogen in the sun's atmosphere.

1860

1861

1862

1860 English nurse Florence Nightingale sets up the first training school for nurses, in London.

1861 English physicist William Crookes uses spectrography to identify the element thallium.

1862 U.S. gunsmith Richard Gatling patents a 10-barrel machine gun.

← A 19th-century drawing shows "animacules" of varying shapes and sizes.

As early as 1546, Italian physician Girolamo Fracastoro suggested in *On Contagion and Contagious Diseases* that germs are the cause of disease. Nobody took much notice, even after 1676, when Dutch scientist Antonie van Leeuwenhoek first saw bacteria, using a omemade microscope. The bacteria were from his own nouth and were probably not disease-carrying.

erm Theory of Disease

hen, in 1840, German pathologist Jacob Henle put orward the idea that infection is caused by parasitic rganisms, the so-called germ theory of disease, which as later proposed independently by French chemist ouis Pasteur. In 1877, German bacteriologist Robert och announced that bacteria could be stained to make nem easier to study under a microscope. Seven years iter, Danish physician Hans Gram extended this idea as means of classifying bacteria, which since then have een dubbed either Gram-positive or Gram-negative

Timeline

1546 Fracastoro suggests germs cause disease
1676 Van Leeuwenhoek discovers bacteria
1840 Henle's germ theory of disease
1884 Gram's stain to classify bacteria
1897 Beijerinck discovers viruses

↓ Antonie van Leeuwenhoek used this handmade microscope to observe the first bacteria.

1863 French chemist Louis Pasteur introduces pasteurization, a process that kills bacteria in food and drink.

1863 The world's first underground railroad, the Metropolitan Line, opens in London.

1863   1864   1865

1863 Swedish chemist Alfred Nobel begins experimenting with the explosive nitroglycerin.

1864 Scottish physicist James Clerk Maxwell publishes Maxwell's equations, which describe mathematically electromagnetic phenomena.

1864 French engineer Pierre Michaux makes the first pedal bicycle.

Viruses

Viruses evaded discovery until the late 19th century. They turned out to have various shapes and to consist of an outer "container" of protein holding a molecule of DNA (deoxyribonucleic acid) or RNA (ribonucleic acid). They cannot multiply outside a living cell; but once they force their way into a cell, they make it rapidly produce more virus particles that break out and invade other cells.

⟹ Shown here are: an adenovirus (A); a bacteriophage (B); and HIV (human immunodeficiency virus).

depending on their capacity to absorb a special stain. Bacteriologists also classify bacteria according to their shapes: coccus (round), bacillus (oval), spirochete (spiral), and so on.

Once biologists knew what bacteria looked like, the hunt was on. Scientists who handled cultures of infectious diseases often put themselves at great risk, but results came quickly. In 1880, German bacteriologist Karl Eberth found the bacillus that causes typhoid. In 1882, fellow German Robert Koch found the bacterium that causes tuberculosis, while German researchers also identified

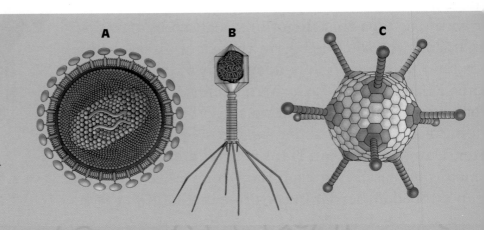

↑ Louis Pasteur used rabbits and other animals in his studies of bacteria.

A   B   C

TIMELINE
1865–1870

KEY:

- Astronomy and Math
- Chemistry and Physics
- Biology and Medicine
- Inventions and Engineering

1865 Austrian monk Gregor Mendel formulates his laws of inheritance.

1865 Belgian chemist Jean Servais Stas devises the first modern tables of atomic weights using oxygen as a standard.

1867 Swedish chemist Alfred Nobel patents dynamite in Britain.

1865   1866   1867

1865 U.S. locksmith Linus Yale perfects the cylinder lock and receives a second patent for it.

1866 Italian astronomer Giovanni Schiaparelli shows that meteor showers are associated with the orbits of comets.

1867 English surgeon Joseph Lister introduc phenol as a disinfecta in the hospital.

e cause of the animal disease glanders. In 1897, Danish
terinarian Bernhard Bang discovered a bacillus that
uses abortion in cattle, and the Japanese bacteriologist
yoshi Shiga found the cause of endemic dysentery.

her Microorganisms

cteria are not the only parasitic microorganisms to
use human diseases. Protozoans, for example, include
e trypanosomes that cause sleeping sickness and
hagas disease, the amebas that result in amebic
sentery, and the Plasmodium parasite responsible for
alaria. Some microscopic fungi produce diseases that
fect the skin or lungs. Most of these microorganisms
ere tracked down by 19th-century microbiologists.
In 1897, Dutch microbiologist Martinus Beijerinck
oved that the microorganism that causes tobacco
osaic disease escapes through a filter that traps
cteria. He had discovered the first virus. Since then,
ruses have been found to be responsible for many
seases in humans, including yellow fever, influenza,
lio, measles, and AIDS (acquired immune deficiency
ndrome). Almost as fast as bacteriologists found
cteria, they developed vaccines against them, so that
ople could be injected and gain immunity. Vaccines
r virus diseases proved more difficult, but now exist
r all the disorders named above except AIDS.

↑ The German Robert
  Koch discovered
the bacterium that
causes tuberculosis. His
breakthrough was the
first step in finding a
cure for one of the
biggest killers of the
19th century.

1868 U.S. engineer
George Westinghouse
designs the air brake for
steam locomotives.

1869 Swiss pathologist Johann
Miescher isolates deoxyribonucleic
acid (DNA), which he calls "nuclein."

1869 The Suez Canal between
the Mediterranean and Red Seas
in Egypt is built by French
engineer Ferdinand de Lesseps.

1868   1869   1870

1868 English astronomer
William Huggins observes
that the star Sirius is
receding from Earth.

1869 Russian chemist
Dmitri Mendeleyev compiles
the first periodic table of
the elements.

1869 The first
transcontinental railroad, the
Union Pacific, is completed.

The Internal Combustion Engin

In the steam engines that powered the Industrial Revolution, external combustion took place. But the internal combustion engine is much more efficient.

→→ German inventor Karl Benz and his assistant ride on an 1885 Benz Motorwagen.

TIMELINE
1870–1875

1870 German chemist Rudolf Fittig makes aromatic hydrocarbons by combining two molecules of a halogen compound in the presence of sodium metal.

1871 German chemist Felix Hoppe-Seyler discovers invertase, the first enzyme to be isolated.

1872 German mathematician Richard Dedekind publishes his theory of irrational numbers.

1870

1871

1872

KEY:

 Astronomy and Math

 Chemistry and Physics

 Biology and Medicine

Inventions and Engineering

1870 German physicist Ernst Abbe introduces the use of his condenser to provide illumination for microscopes.

1871 U.S. engineer Simon Ingersoll invents a pneumatic rock drill.

1871 English inventor James Starley patents the "penny-farthing" bicycle.

The Belgian engineer Étienne Lenoir made the first successful engine to burn fuel internally in 1859. It [ra]n on coal gas, which was mixed with air and sucked [in]to the cylinder by the movement of a piston. It [pr]oduced about 1 horsepower and worked in two jerky [st]ages with the help of a heavy flywheel.

[T]he First Engines

[In] 1862, French engineer Alphonse Beau de Rochas [pa]tented an engine that worked in four stages, or [st]rokes. He did not build an actual [en]gine, and the idea was later taken [u]p by a self-taught German engineer, [N]ikolaus Otto. In 1876, Otto made [hi]s first horizontal four-stroke gas [en]gine; it ran at about 180 rpm and [pr]oduced 3 horsepower. The four-[st]roke cycle is still the basis of today's [m]odern engines.

[ ] Otto's engine still used coal gas. In [18]67, the Austrian engineer Siegfried [M]arcus invented a carburetor that [va]porized liquid gasoline and mixed it with air. Two [G]erman engineers, Karl Benz and Gottlieb Daimler, [in]dependently made the first gasoline-burning internal [co]mbustion engines in 1885. Both engines were used to [de]velop motor vehicles. Daimler's engine ran at 900 rpm

This German stamp celebrates Rudolf Diesel, who invented the diesel engine in 1892.

1873 French engineer Amédée Bollée constructs a steam-powered car.

1874 U.S. physician Andrew Still founds osteopathy, which uses manipulation of bones and joints to treat diseases.

1875 A safe loading level for ships, called the Plimsoll line, is introduced in Britain, and soon taken up everywhere.

1873   1874   1875

1873 Scottish physicist James Clerk Maxwell publishes his electromagnetic theory of light: that light is a form of electromagnetic radiation (like radio waves and X-rays).

1874 Irish physicist George Stoney coins the phrase "electrine" for the fundamental unit of electricty; later he changes it to "electron."

The Two-Stroke Engine

In a two-stroke engine, the piston acts as a valve. On the upstroke, the piston compresses the fuel-and-air mixture, which is ignited by a spark from the spark plug. The piston closes off the exhaust port. The explosion forces the piston down, the downstroke. Exhaust gases escape via the uncovered port, and as the piston rises again, fresh fuel-and-air is sucked in through the open inlet port.

→ The up-and-down motion of the piston is turned into rotary motion by a crankshaft.

and used a red-hot platinum tube to ignite the fuel and a carburetor that had been invented by his business partner, German engineer Wilhelm Maybach. The engine built by Benz was slower than Daimler's (only 250 rpm) and produced less than 1 horsepower, but the car he used it in had many modern features, including coil ignition powered by a battery and a distributor.

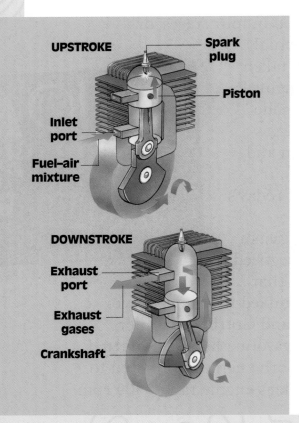

UPSTROKE — Spark plug
— Piston
Inlet port
Fuel-air mixture

DOWNSTROKE
Exhaust port
Exhaust gases
Crankshaft

Improving Engines

By the end of the 19th century, the scientific principle of engines was being analyzed. If a suitable fuel–air mixture is hot and compressed enough, it will combust spontaneously. The Englishman Herbert Stuart patented the first example of a compression-ignition engine in 1890. Two years later, a German inventor, Rudolf Diesel, patented a similar engine and demonstrated it in 1897. Since then, this type of engine has been known as a diesel engine.

TIMELINE
1875–1880

KEY:

Astronomy and Math

s and ring

1875 French physicist Jules Violle measures the solar constant—the amount of the Sun's energy that reaches the top of Earth's atmosphere.

1876 German botanist Eduard Strasburger describes mitosis, the process of cell division into two identical cells.

1877 German bacteriolog Robert Koch develops a w of staining bacteria to ma them easier to study.

1875

1876

1877

1876 Scottish-born U.S. engineer Alexander Graham Bell patents the telephone.

1876 U.S. librarian Melvil Dewey introduces the Dewey Decimal System for cataloging library books.

1876 German engineer Nikolaus Otto builds a four-stroke internal combustion engine fueled by coal gas.

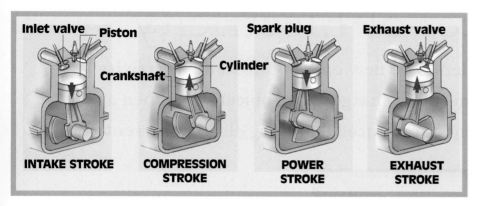

Inlet valve Piston Spark plug Exhaust valve

Crankshaft Cylinder

INTAKE STROKE COMPRESSION STROKE POWER STROKE EXHAUST STROKE

↑ This diagram shows the four strokes of a standard four-stroke engine.

The Four-Stroke Engine

In a four-stroke engine, on the intake stroke, the inlet valve opens as the piston moves down. This sucks a fuel-and-air mixture into the cylinder. On the compression stroke, the inlet valve closes and the piston rises, compressing the fuel and air. During the power stroke, the spark plug ignites the fuel, which explodes, and the hot gases force the piston down. On the fourth stroke, the exhaust valve opens to allow gases to escape while the piston rises.

A diesel engine has several advantages. It uses a less refined, and therefore cheaper, fuel than gasoline. The engine needs no spark plugs or associated ignition system and is 35 percent efficient in fuel consumption, compared with 25 percent for the best gasoline engines. Both figures are far off the theoretical maximum efficiency of 67 percent for a perfect heat engine.

The early gasoline (and all diesel) engines were examples of reciprocating engines. There were some "rotary" gasoline engines, developed very successfully as power plants for propeller-driven aircraft.

In 1929, German engineer Felix Wankel patented a revolutionary internal combustion engine that was truly rotatory. The first prototype was made in 1956. A Wankel engine has a rotor that rotates inside a "cylinder" shaped like a fat figure eight.

1878 U.S. inventor Thomas Alva Edison demonstrates his electric lightbulb.

1879 English inventor Henry Lawson invents the "safety" bicycle, driven by a chain to the rear wheel—the model for all modern bicycles.

1878   1879   1880

1878 U.S. astronomer Asaph Hall discovers the two moons of Mars, Phobos and Deimos.

1879 U.S. chemists discover saccharin, an artificial sweetener 2,000 times sweeter than sugar.

1880 French chemist Louis Pasteur identifies the Streptococcus bacterium.

Sources of Electricity

Before 1800, scientists knew only about static electricity— a positive or negative charge on an object—but then an Italian nobleman produced a moving electric current.

→ Volta shows off his battery, or voltaic pile, to Napoleon I, the emperor of France.

In 1791, Italian physician Luigi Galvani reported what he called "animal electricity." Dissecting a dead frog, he found the animal's muscles twitched when he touched them with two different metals. In 1800, Count Alessandro Volta, an Italian physicist, replaced the animal tissue with a cardboard disk soaked in salt solution. He put a piece of copper or silver on one side and zinc on the other side. Wires connected to the metal plates carried an electric current. Volta found he could obtain higher voltages by making a stack of such disks

TIMELINE
1880–1885

KEY:
Astronomy and Math
and ng

1880 Scottish astronomer George Forbes predicts the existence of "Planet X" orbiting beyond Neptune: Pluto is discovered in 1930.

1881 U.S. astronomer Henry Draper takes the first photographs of comets.

1882 German bacteriologist Robert Koch discovers the bacterium that causes tuberculosis and, in 1883, that causes cholera.

1880

1881

1882

1880 German bacteriologist Karl Eberth discovers the bacterium that causes typhoid fever.

1881 English physicist J.J. Thompson predicts that an object's mass changes when it becomes electrically charged.

1882 The first U.S. steam powered electricity-generating plant opens in New York City.

to form a voltaic battery (the first true battery). Today, scientists call such a battery a primary cell. The pieces of metal are electrodes, and the solution between them is an electrolyte. In 1836, English chemist John Daniell produced a more efficient type of primary cell. Its current was steadier than Volta's cell and overcame the problem of polarization—a build-up of hydrogen bubbles on the copper electrode that eventually causes the voltaic pile to stop working.

Volta's Successors

The Leclanché cell, a battery invented in 1866 by French engineer Georges Leclanché, also avoids polarization. It used an electrolyte of ammonium chloride solution. It produces about 1.5 volts. Today's common type of dry battery has the same system.

The German chemist Robert Bunsen made a zinc–carbon primary cell; using acid electrolytes, it produces 1.9 volts. The cadmium cell, invented in 1893 by English-born American electrical engineer Edward Weston, produces

<< Luigi Galvani discovered that a frog's limbs twitched if he applied two types of metal to create an electric charge.

1884 U.S.-born English inventor Hiram Maxim makes the first fully automatic machine gun.

1884 U.S. engineer Frank Sprague—"the father of electric railway traction"—forms the Sprague Electric Railway and Motor Company.

1883   1884   1885

1883 Belgian engineer Étienne Lenoir invents the spark plug (for internal combustion engines).

1884 German physiologist Max Rubner shows that the body makes use of carbohydrates, fats, and proteins in order to produce energy.

1884 German astronomer Max Wolf discover's Wolf's comet, with a period of just seven years.

The Primary Cell Battery

A primary cell, such as the dry battery for a flashlight (below right), can be used only until its chemicals run out, when it has to be thrown away (carefully). In this type of cell, the electrolyte is a paste of ammonium chloride and gum. The zinc cathode forms the case of the battery, and manganese dioxide and carbon surround the central carbon anode.

→ This battery uses carbon and zinc for the anode and cathode, respectively.

1.0186 volts, and in 1908 the scientific community accepted it as a standard of voltage. It is known as the Weston standard cell. English electrical engineer Josiah Clark invented the Clark standard cell 21 years earlier, in 1872, using zinc instead of cadmium.

A primary cell stops working when it is fully discharged. A secondary cell (or storage cell, or accumulator) can be recharged. In 1859, French chemist Gaston Planté devised the lead–acid accumulator. It is the earliest and most commonly used battery, used in most cars. It has one electrode (or "plate") of lead and one of lead covered with lead oxide, which dip into a sulfuric acid electrolyte. Another type, the alkaline nickel–iron accumulator, or Ni–Fe cell, was invented in 1900 by American inventor Thomas Edison.

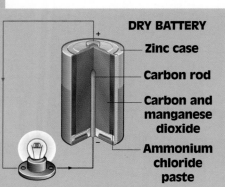

↑ The Leclanché cell used the same principles as most modern dry batteries.

DRY BATTERY

- **Zinc case**
- **Carbon rod**
- **Carbon and manganese dioxide**
- **Ammonium chloride paste**

TIMELINE
1885–1890

1885 Austrian doctor Sigmund Freud develops psychoanalysis as a diagnostic procedure.

1885 French chemist Louis Pasteur produces a vaccine against rabies.

1887 German physicist Heinrich Hertz detects radio waves.

KEY:

- Astronomy and Math
- Chemistry and Physics
- Biology and Medicine
- Inventions and Engineering

1885

1886

1887

1885 U.S. architect William Jenney builds the world's first skyscraper, a steel-framed building in Chicago.

1885 U.S. electrical engineer William Stanley invents the transformer.

1886 U.S. chemist John Pemberton invents Coca-Cola.

When any accumulator becomes discharged, it can be connected to a supply of DC (direct current) and recharged. For example, as a car's motor is running, the battery is continually recharged.

Both primary and secondary cells convert chemical energy into electrical energy. In doing so, they "consume" materials in the electrodes or electrolyte. A fuel cell, however, converts the chemical energy of a fuel directly into electrical energy. The first fuel cell, which "consumed" hydrogen and oxygen gases, was demonstrated in 1839 by Welsh physicist and judge William Grove.

Volta is the best remembered scientist. He gave his name to the volt, adopted in 1905 as the SI unit of electric potential.

↓ Car batteries are secondary cells, or accumulators, that are charged by the engine.

Secondary Cell

A secondary cell, or accumulator, can be recharged. It has lead and lead-oxide electrodes in a sulfuric acid electrolyte. In use, sulfate ions react with the lead cathode to produce lead sulfate and release electrons. To recharge the accumulator, current from an outside source is passed through the battery in the opposite direction. This reverses the reactions at the electrodes, reforming lead and lead oxide. The accumulator is then ready for use again.

ACCUMULATOR ON CHARGE

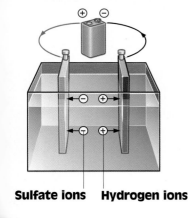

Sulfate ions   Hydrogen ions

ACCUMULATOR IN USE

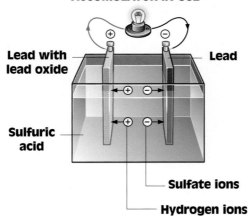

Lead with lead oxide

Lead

Sulfuric acid

Sulfate ions

Hydrogen ions

1889 Swedish physical chemist Svante Arrhenius derives the Arrhenius equation, a way of calculating the speed of a chemical reaction.

1889 U.S. astronomer Edward Barnard takes the first photographs of the Milky Way (our galaxy).

1888   1889   1890

1888 Danish astronomer Johan Dreyer publishes a new catalog of nebulae and star clusters.

1889 The Eiffel Tower is completed in Paris, France.

1890 U.S. inventor Herman Hollerith invents a punch-card reader (for recording census results).

The Elusive Electron

Today, every science student knows the importance of an electron in understanding electricity and atomic physics. A century ago, things were very different.

↑ Seven of J. J. Thomson's students subsequently received Nobel prizes.

TIMELINE
1890–1895

KEY:

- Astronomy and Math
- Chemistry and Physics
- Biology and Medicine
- Inventions and Engineering

1890 German bacteriologists produce antitoxins against the diseases diphtheria and tetanus.

1891 German engineer Otto Lilienthal makes a steerable human-carrying glider.

1892 English scientist Francis Galton argues that no two people have the same fingerprints, and that fingerprints can be used in crime investigation.

1890 — 1891 — 1892

1890 Russian physiologist begins experimenting with dogs to study how nerve impulses stimulate digestive secretion in the stomach.

1892 German bacteriologist Robert Koch introduces filtration of water to control a cholera epidemic in Hamburg, Germany.

ntil the end of the 19th century, discoveries in physics had left unanswered questions such as: bjects can hold a charge of static electricity, but what rm does the charge take? What are the electric current arges that flow along a conductor and are they fferent from the electrostatic ones? A high voltage cross the plates of a vacuum tube produces cathode ys, but what are the rays made of? And if matter is ade of atoms, what are atoms made of?

he First Answers

he answer to these questions came from one invention –the vacuum pump. Scientists could now remove most f the air from any apparatus. Around 1850, the erman laboratory equipment anufacturer Heinrich Geissler aled metal plates inside a glass acuum tube containing traces of gas. He connected the plates to a urce of high-voltage electricity nd obtained pretty lighting effects the gas glowed. Geissler tubes ere used by two erman physicists: lius Plücker in 359 and Johann

→» This plaque marks the site of the Cavendish Laboratory in Cambridge, England.

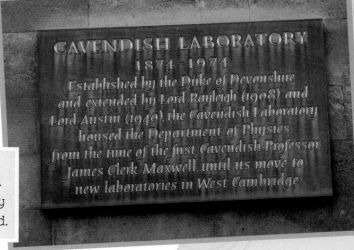

CAVENDISH LABORATORY
1874–1974
Established by the Duke of Devonshire and extended by Lord Rayleigh (1908) and Lord Austin (1940), the Cavendish Laboratory housed the Department of Physics from the time of the first Cavendish Professor James Clerk Maxwell, until its move to new laboratories in West Cambridge

Timeline

1850 Geissler tubes invented

1874 Stoney predicts existence of electrons

1879 Crookes suggests cathode rays are particles

1891 Electron named

1895 Perrin proves cathode rays are made up of negative charges

1897 Electron discovered

1893 African American surgeon Daniel Williams performs the first open-heart surgery.

1893 The French Lumière brothers invent a motion-picture camera.

1895 Swedish and Scottish chemists independently discover helium on Earth (previously it was only known in the sun's spectrum).

1893   1894   1895

1893 German engineer Rudolf Diesel first builds a compression-ignition engine (diesel engine).

1894 U.S. astronomer Percival Lowell sets up a private observatory at Flagstaff, Arizona, to search for the ninth planet.

1895 German physicist Wilhelm Röntgen takes the first X-ray.

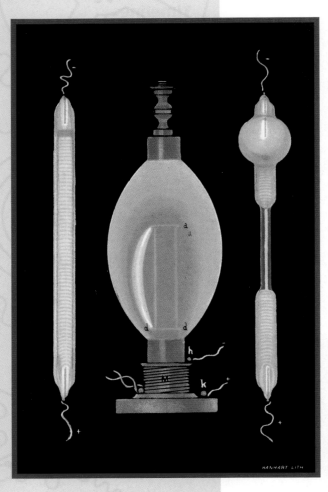

Geissler tubes are glass tubes or bulbs with most of the air pumped out of them.

Hittorf in 1869. They claimed the light resulted from "rays" traveling in the Geissler tube. In 1879, English physicist William Crookes confirmed this and suggested the "rays" may be particles. Sixteen years later, French physicist Jean Perrin deflected these cathode rays.

Thomson and Cathode Rays

Then along came the English physicist J. J. Thomson. At age 14, he trained as a railroad engineer, then won a scholarship to Cambridge University, graduating in 1880. He worked in the Cavendish Laboratory, and became head of the laboratory in 1884.

Thomson deflected cathode rays with electric and magnetic fields, measured their speed (proving they travel more slowly than light waves), and figured out the ratio of their charge (e) to their mass (m). Thomson deduced that cathode rays must consist of minute negatively charged particles. He announced the discovery of the first subatomic particles in 1897, and in 189_ found they have a mass equal to about one two-thousandth of the mass of a hydrogen atom. In 1874, George Stoney had predicted their existence. In 1891, h_ named them "electrons." The electron was the unit of electricity responsible for electrostatic charges. It

TIMELINE
1895–1900

1896 French physicist Henri Becquerel discovers radioactivity.

1896 New Zealand-born British physicist Ernest Rutherford describes and names alpha particles (which are helium nuclei) and beta particles (which are electrons).

KEY:

- Astronomy and Math
- Chemistry and Physics
- Biology and Medicine
- Inventions and Engineering

1895   1896   1897

1895 U.S. inventor King Gillette has the idea for the disposable double-edge razor blade.

1897 German physicist Ferdinand Braun invents the cathode-ray tube, later used in radar and TV sets.

1897 English physicist J.J. Thompson identifies the electron, the first subatomic particle.

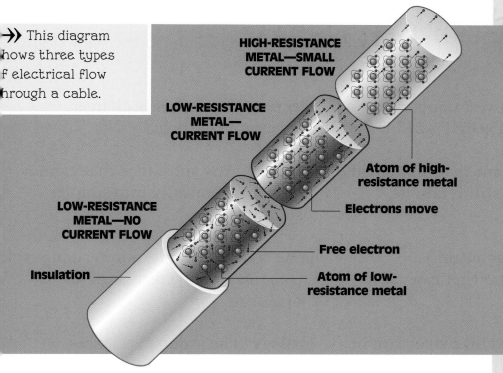

→ This diagram shows three types of electrical flow through a cable.

HIGH-RESISTANCE METAL—SMALL CURRENT FLOW

LOW-RESISTANCE METAL—CURRENT FLOW

LOW-RESISTANCE METAL—NO CURRENT FLOW

Atom of high-resistance metal

Electrons move

Free electron

Atom of low-resistance metal

Insulation

Electricity Flow

Electrons occur in all atoms. In most metals—such as the copper in electric cable—many electrons leave their atoms to form a "sea" of free electrons (bottom of diagram). When a voltage is applied (middle section), the free electrons move to form an electric current. Copper is said to have low resistance. A metal with high resistance, such as tungsten used in electric heaters, has few free electrons (top section). A voltage causes only a small current, and the metal becomes hot.

ecame clear that a flow of electrons along a conductor as an electric current. Since electrons come from the etal of the cathode, they must be part of all atoms. Thomson studied canal rays, which led in 1912 to a ay of separating charged particles. In 1919, the English hysicist Francis Aston developed the mass spectograph. Then Thomson retired in 1919, he was succeeded by s former assistant, Ernest Rutherford. Rutherford ventually proposed a structure for the atom that cluded the atomic nucleus. Seven of Thomson's sistants won Nobel prizes. He received it in 1906.

1898 English physician Ronald Ross finds the microorganism plasmodia, which causes malaria, in the stomach of a mosquito; he argues that mosquito bites transfer the parasite to humans.

1900 Austrian-born U.S. pathologist Karl Landsteiner discovers the A, B, and O blood groups and their intercompatability.

1898

1899

1900

898 French chemists ierre and Marie Curie iscover the elements olonium and radium.

1898 English physiologist John Langley identifies the autonomic nervous system, which controls involuntary muscles and glands.

1900 German physicist Max Planck proposes the quantum theory: that radiation is emitted in separate "packets," or quanta.

Glossary

absolute zero The lowest temperature possible (equal to −459.67°F/−273.15°C).

atom The smallest unit that matter can be divided into and still retain its chemical identity.

bacteria (Singular bacterium) Microcopic organisms that can cause disease.

chromosome A threadlike structure in the nucleus of a living cell that carries the genetic information.

compound chemical A substance in which molecules are made up from atoms of more than one element.

conductor Any substance that allows an electric current, heat, or sound to pass through it.

ecology The study of the relationship of plants and animals to their environment and to each other.

electric current A flow of electrons through a conductor.

electromagnetism The phenomenon by which magnetic fields can be produced by the flow of electrons in an electronic current.

electron A negatively charged subatomic particle.

element Any substance that cannot be split chemically into simpler substances.

gene The basic unit of inheritance that controls a characteristic of an organism.

geology The group of sciences concerned with the study of Earth, including its structure, long-term history, composition, and origins.

microorganism The general term for any living organism that is invisible to the naked eye but visible under a microscope.

photosynthesis The process by which green plants convert light energy from the sun.

subatomic particle Any particle that is smaller than an atom.

vaccine A preparation containing viruses or other microorganisms introduced into the body to build up immunity against infectious disease.

virus A tiny parasitic organism that can reproduce only inside the cell of its host.

Further Reading

Books

Bankston, John. *Gregor Mendel and the Discovery of the Gene.* Hockessin, DE: Mitchell Lane Publishers, 2004.

Baxter, Roberta. *Michael Faraday and the Nature of Electricity.* Greensboro, NC: Morgan Reynolds Publishing, 2008.

Goodhue, Thomas W. *Curious Bones: Mary Anning and the Birth of Paleontology.* Greensboro, NC: Morgan Reynolds Publishing, 2002.

Lassieur, Allison. *Louis Pasteur: Revolutionary Scientist.* New York: Franklin Watts, 2005.

MacDonald, Fiona, and Mark Bergin. *Inside the* Beagle *with Charles Darwin.* New York: Enchanted Lion Books, 2005.

Pasachoff, Naomi. *Ernest Rutherford: Father of Nuclear Science.* Berkeley Heights, NJ: Enslow Publishers, 2005.

Sherman, Josepha. *J. J. Thomson and the Discovery of Electrons.* Hockessin, DE: Mitchell Lane Publishers, 2005.

Sis, Peter. *The Tree of Life: Charles Darwin.* New York: Farrar, Strauss, and Giroux, 2003.

Van Gorp, Lynn. *Gregor Mendel: Genetics Pioneer.* Mankato, MN: Compass Point Books, 2008.

White, Katherine. *Mendeleyev and the Periodic Table.* New York: Rosen Publishing Group, 2004.

Zannos, Susan. *Dmitri Mendeleyev and the Periodic Table.* Hockessin, DE: Mitchell Lane Publishers, 2004.

Zannos, Susan. *Michael Faraday and the Discovery of Electromagnetism.* Hockessin, DE: Mitchell Lane Publishers, 2004.

Web Sites

http://inventors.about.com/cs/inventors alphabet/a/electricity.htm
About.com's page on the discovery of electricity, with many links.

http://www.periodicvideos.com/#
The University of Nottingham's interactive video periodic table.

http://www.amnh.org/exhibitions/ darwin/
The American Museum of Natural History's page on Darwin's life and work.

Index